THE GIFT OF PLEASANT HILL

THE GIFT OF PLEASANT HILL

SHAKER COMMUNITY IN KENTUCKY

Photographs by
JAMES ARCHAMBEAULT

Introduction by
THOMAS D. CLARK

PLEASANT HILL PRESS

Shakertown at Pleasant Hill, Kentucky, Inc., wishes to thank the following individuals for their contribution toward the publication of this book: Larrie Spier Curry, Susanna Massie, Herbert Sparrow, Marcheta Sparrow, William T. Young, chairman of the board of trustees, and Susan Jackson Keig, design consultant.

Photographs on pages 53, 114-115, 146 and the dust jacket, back cover, were originally published in the book *Kentucky II,* by James Archambeault and Thomas D. Clark, and are used with permission of Graphic Arts Center Publishing Company, Portland, Oregon.

Library of Congress Cataloging-in-Publication Data

Archambeault, James.
    The gift of Pleasant Hill: Shaker community in Kentucky /
photographs by James Archambeault; introduction by Thomas D. Clark.
        p.   cm.
    Includes index.
    ISBN 0-9629116-0-7 (hardcover) : $38.50
    1. Shakers—Kentucky—Pleasant Hill—Pictorial works. 2. Pleasant
Hill (Ky.)—Church history—Pictorial works. I. Title.
BX9768.P6A72   1991
976.9'33—dc20   91-19274
                                                              CIP

Photograph on title page: *Meeting House, where Sunday worship services were held.*

PREFACE

Surely one of the most photographed sites in Kentucky is the Shaker Village of Pleasant Hill. The land atop the hill falls gently from east to west where more than thirty original Shaker structures remain as an enduring statement of Shaker values. The rolling countryside, the dramatic Kentucky River valley, and the serene village possess exceptional beauty and unlimited opportunity for photographers. So thought Earl D. Wallace, Sr. (1898-1990), first chairman of the board of trustees for Shakertown.

Three decades ago, a group of concerned Kentuckians spearheaded by Mr. Wallace founded a nonprofit, educational corporation to bring Pleasant Hill back to life as a living historical museum. Beginning in 1961, the new organization under Chairman Wallace began the arduous task of acquiring original Shaker lands, restoring their buildings, and devising programs to attract visitors to this once-prosperous site.

Even then Earl Wallace envisioned a book of rich color images portraying the many visual facets of Pleasant Hill. Waiting patiently until the village restoration was nearly complete, Earl Wallace asked noted photographer James Archambeault to undertake a book project for Shakertown. No stranger to Pleasant Hill, Mr. Archambeault had been commissioned by our staff several years ago to do a series of exquisite postcards of village scenes. In the spring of 1989, Archambeault began this book project and since that time has documented the changing seasons of the year and the essence of the site with the creative eye of the artist-photographer.

To add historical perspective to this work, Mr. Wallace invited Dr. Thomas D. Clark, recently named Kentucky's Laureate Historian for life, to write an introduction to the book. A remarkable similarity of style is apparent when one looks at the rich color plates of James Archambeault and reads the lyrical text of Tom Clark.

Regrettably, Earl Wallace did not live to see this book in print. It is in his memory that we present *The Gift of Pleasant Hill*. We hope others will become interested in Pleasant Hill and find this site a true gift from the Shakers.

Pleasant Hill
February 1, 1991

JAMES CHESTON THOMAS
President and Chief Executive Officer
Shakertown at Pleasant Hill, Ky, Inc.

ACKNOWLEDGMENTS

There are many people to whom I owe thanks. These include the interpreters and administrative staff who assisted me unselfishly and endured my unannounced visits with patience and good humor. Their detailed knowledge and feeling for the life of the Shakers provided me with surprising insights.

To my wife, Lee, whose personal vision helped me sort through the many ideas, words and photographs that comprise this book. She was with me on many of my journeys to Shakertown. Her eyes saw things mine did not. She is a part of this book.

To Susan Jackson Keig, award-winning graphic designer who has worked closely with Shakertown for over twenty years. She has given me a new sense of aesthetics and I am honored to have worked with her.

To Ed Nickels, former curator of collections, who first took me through the Village in 1987 and introduced me to many photographic possibilities. His life was taken far too early for a person of his genius and goodness.

To Jim Thomas, whose dedication and guidance as president of Pleasant Hill have provided integrity and commitment. More than anyone, his vision is the thread that gives lasting continuity to the spirit of Shakertown and the people who make up the life of the Village.

To Larrie Curry and Marcheta Sparrow, who contributed their creative energy over countless hours, preparing manuscript for captions, jacket and biographies. Their frontline knowledge of the Shaker Village and its history contributed greatly to this volume.

To Thomas Clark, a true gentleman and friend, one of Kentucky's premier thinkers and its foremost historian. He has been my collaborator in two previous books, *Kentucky* and *Kentucky II.* It has been my great fortune to be associated with him.

The Shakers are not here: but the shafts of sunlight flooding their vacant rooms cast the same patterns that warmed them, woke them, lighted their days and their work. To be in these rooms is to see and capture the light they saw, to witness part of the world in which they lived.

JAMES ARCHAMBEAULT

INTRODUCTION

For countless centuries the waters of the Kentucky River slowly cut a serpentine channel through the great limestone dome of Central Kentucky, creating miles of dramatic stone-faced palisades. It was here a group of newly-converted members of the Society of Believers, or Shakers, came in August, 1805, to establish a tiny community on Elisha Thomas' 140-acre farm along the Shawnee Run Creek. The site, located on a plateau above the ancient and meandering river, was strategically within the sprawling triangle of Kentucky's historic beginnings. Not far away to the southwest was Harrod's Town, the state's first permanent settlement dating from 1774. Forty miles upstream on the south bank of the Kentucky River was Boonesborough, site of the Transylvania Land Company's speculative venture, while north of the river were the town of Lexington and the armed fort of Bryant's Station.

The land atop the Mercer County plateau the Shakers chose has a rolling surface—some of it fertile and some of it dipping into ravines and coves—that gives it a diversity of nature. The Shakers' newly-settled land, like other farmlands across Central Kentucky, required an enormous amount of human labor to clear forest cover and to lay outcropping rocks into winding stone fences.

Nevertheless, the land rewarded its industrious and thrifty Shaker inhabitants generously. The meadows were ideally suited for grazing cattle and sheep; the woodland coves productive of mast, the fruit of oak and beech trees used to fatten range hogs.

The Shakers aggressively tamed this wilderness and formed an impressive, complex farmstead where they, unlike many of their worldly neighbors, built with an eye focused on the future as well as aesthetics. Even their simplest outbuildings revealed an honesty of design and workmanship. The integrity of the buildings, combined with the beauty of the land, created a rare aura of pastoral and sylvan beauty. Here, as much as any place in North America, the Shakers could realize the age-old dream of rural peace and plenty.

However, there appeared to be little of the Society covenants that would appeal religiously or emotionally to the rural Kentucky mind in the early 1800s. Shaker religious beliefs and theology were, at best, highly unorthodox and complex. They combined the personal beliefs of the sect's founder, Mother Ann Lee, and some tenets of the Church of England with a generous dose of Quakerism. There were three basic tenets to the Shaker religion: celibacy, public confessions of sins, and the second coming of Jesus Christ, but this time in female form.

To comprehend the Shaker faith and community, it is necessary to know something of Ann Lee's personal background. She was born in 1736 in the grim city of Manchester, England. In her early youth she worked in a textile factory and later in an infirmary and a fur trimming shop. She married a crude blacksmith and bore him four children, all of whom died in infancy.

Ann Lee, who was illiterate, became associated with a separatist group known as "Shaking" Quakers. In her religious fervor she disrupted a Church of England service, for which she was imprisoned. While in prison, she received a spiritual visitation which revealed that Christ would return as a female. Once free of jail, she gathered about her a group of Believers who accompanied her to North America in 1774 (at the same time that James Harrod was leading a party up the Kentucky River to settle Harrod's Town) to establish a celibate community where her beliefs could be practiced uninterrupted.

After two years and numerous difficulties, the new order, officially known as "The United Society of Believers in Christ's Second Appearing," settled on a boggy tract of land at Niskayuna near Albany, New York. They later established the community at New Lebanon on the New York-Massachusetts border. The Society depended upon proselyting to the faith to gather in new members and it was from these centers that the Shakers began an active crusade to found other communities.

Due in part to the Great Revivals of the early nineteenth century, the emissaries of the Society of Believers were able to proselytize members in Kentucky and persuade a rugged pioneer people to dissolve their marriages, surrender possession of their land, and accept a regulated mode of living. Perhaps the converts saw in the organization of the Shaker community elements of safety in numbers and a collected presence of the "final day" as indicated in the Society's covenant.

Forty-four Believers assembled on the Thomas farm in December, 1806, to sign a family covenant, dissolving former ties and separating themselves from the world. Adjacent land was purchased as their membership increased. In the fall of 1808 they moved from Shawnee Run to a location approximately one and one-half miles east. They named this new site Pleasant Hill.

Unlike most communal societies in nineteenth-century America, the Shakers were able to live apart from the world, yet be very much a part of it. The designation "world," as it appeared frequently in the village journals, was no more than an abstraction which encompassed the vast area beyond the local confines of the faith. Although they strove to be separate from outside influences, the Shakers would have been hard-pressed to maintain their comfortable way of life during the flourishing decades of the mid-nineteenth century without access to the world as a market for garden seeds, brooms, crafts, farm produce, and livestock. And, with Pleasant Hill sitting astride the major north and south post roads through Kentucky, the world literally flowed past their doorstep.

The great curving sweep of the Kentucky River and the steep rocky face of the palisades gave Pleasant Hill farmlands an insulated barrier to the north and east, while on the other boundaries lay open farm country. This geographic setting symbolically reflected the Shakers' approach to life itself. In this semi-isolated corner of Kentucky, they were able to exercise close disciplinary control over the order and its converts, yet reach out at will into the world.

For over three-quarters of a century the saga of the Kentucky River runs through Shaker journals in phrases of eloquent esteem. It became as intimate a part of the history of Pleasant Hill as the land itself. From its limestone shoulders the Shakers chiseled great blocks of stone and from its forested shores they harvested ever-increasing volumes of virgin timber with which to construct their buildings. Ingeniously, the young Shaker architect Micajah Burnett and his fellow Believers shaped these materials into solid foundations, classical walls, wood framing, and graceful stairways. Today, standing as sturdily after a century-and-a-half as the day they were lifted into place, the family dwellings, the Meeting House, the shops, and the farm buildings are stately documentation of the skill with which the builders converted raw materials into structures of grace, beauty and durability. On days when the Kentucky River thrusts up a gossamer of mist, Pleasant Hill, with its collection of harmonious and simple buildings, assumes the ethereal appearance of a floating island.

The village scribe sat atop his stool and observed the events of the village which went on about him, leaving us with an often-detailed record of the everyday activities and practices, both mundane and exalted, of this religious order. Outsiders called them "Shakers" because of the whirling dances that were a part of their religious ceremonies. While they came to accept this appellation, they referred to themselves as the Believers throughout the journals.

The Pleasant Hill journals reflect a highly complacent and provincial way of life for the Believers. In this respect, they followed the pattern of most rural Americans during the first decades of the nineteenth century. If there was one dominant theme of these Shaker journals, it was that of work and the expenditure of enormous amounts of human energy. During nearly three-quarters of the nineteenth century, Pleasant Hill was a veritable beehive of work-a-day activity. It was no place for a laggard, and perhaps the work and daily life regimen caused many Believers to return to the world. This work ethic grew from the roots of Shakerism and Mother Ann's words, "Put your hands to work and your hearts to God."

The village journals are litanies of work and industry interspersed with times of relaxation. For instance, on August 3, 1839, William Verbreke began harvesting wheat, Jinny Runyon finished her carpets, workers burned bricks, and others were occupied almost continually in constructing and repairing buildings. In October of that year, villagers gathered, cut, and dried apples, finished the brickwork on the office, shingled its roof, and cleaned out the cisterns for the winter. During the winter months much of the work was taken indoors, where brethren and sisters broke flax, spun thread, and wove large quantities of cloth both for the village and for sale. Craftsmen made brooms, cooper's ware, and fans for sale. All hands dried and packed garden seeds, dug walnut roots, and gathered madder for dyeing cloth, stockings, and sweaters. During August, 1851, the younger sisters sat up all night cutting peaches and apples in preparation for the dry house. In fact, they cut fruit for more than a week that season. For relaxation from the task, they hiked to the Kentucky River cliffs.

Shaker sisters busied themselves, in and out of season, cleaning the buildings, laying carpets, and refurbishing the interiors. The addition of every new structure added a responsibility for its care and upkeep. The craftsmen who worked in the shops were busy year-round making furniture, inventing labor-saving devices, making brooms, and repairing implements and utensils.

The theme of a community striving to live off its natural resources also ran through the journals of the village scribe like a scarlet thread woven through a drab bolt of worsted. The Shakers of Pleasant Hill were able to extract an abundant living from the land. No other nineteenth-century Kentuckians were more raptly attuned to the rhythms of the land and the seasonal changes. Their lives were synchronized to the unfolding and dormancies of nature. The burgeoning spring months, the maturing of fruits and vegetables in the summer, and the creeping southward of fall and winter chills set the schedule for life at Pleasant Hill.

During the early spring of 1857 the collected families finished shearing their sheep, harvesting 2775 pounds of wool. The sisters were busy unreeling silk produced by their silkworms and the brethren busied themselves with lambing, the breeding of hogs, horses and cattle (the Shakers had a solid reputation as breeders of livestock and often attended Central Kentucky livestock shows and fairs as exhibitors or buyers).

The first warming of the soil found them in the fields preparing for planting crops. By late November the frost had laid the fields dormant, and the time was right for killing hogs. Once the smokehouses were filled, the families set to carding wool, spinning and weaving woolens, worsted and linen. There was never a moment when the work at Pleasant Hill was done, the plows stood idle, the grain cradles empty, or the mill wheel stilled.

I n the truest archaeological-anthropological sense they were gatherers. The village journals seem to indicate that some member of the Pleasant Hill Society knew the whereabouts of every patch of blackberries, crabapple trees, walnut trees, and every other edible fruit or nut. They were experts at locating dyestuffs, in identifying medicinal herbs, and finding the oak-studded slopes which yielded rich mast falls. Truly, the land atop the Kentucky River plateau was a "Pleasant Hill."

Perpetual movement was a central characteristic of the Shakers. There was little that was austere or cloistered about their way of life. Shaker traders, identifiable by their broad-brimmed hats and turtleback coats of coarse worsted, traveled far, frequently setting off down the Kentucky River on flatboats to reach markets for their produce, flat brooms, preserves, garden seeds, and craft items.

There was constant social exchange between Pleasant Hill and other Shaker communities. Village journals leave the impression that visitors from other villages were often present at Pleasant Hill or that parties from Pleasant Hill were en route to visit other villages. There are frequent journal notations of the elders and eldresses going out to meet incoming visitors. Perhaps the most unusual of visitors were the ethereal ones who turned up on occasion. Among these were Mother Ann Lee, George Washington, many of the Hebrew prophets, and delegations of American Indians. These visitations were recorded as soberly as if they had actually been made by flesh and blood individuals.

Although the sect's governing body banned the use of coffee and tea and limited pork consumption in 1843, the Pleasant Hill Shakers continued to eat well. They slaughtered cattle for meat, preserved homegrown fruits and vegetables, and produced their own flour and meal. As a result of their resolve to give up "all strong drink, tea, coffee. . . ." they experimented with various fruits and cereals to produce new beverages. The village cooks prepared plentiful amounts of food which were plain but good. Dining, like every other communal activity, was well-ordered. The brethren and sisters ate at separate tables on either side of the dining room. Meals were served promptly: breakfast at six (six-thirty in the winter), dinner at noon, supper at six in the evening. On occasion, the families observed what they called a time of "releasement," when they would go on a picnic. One such event was noted in a September 1, 1842, journal entry: "the Centre family walked out the second time and got their dinner and supper in the woods."

The Pleasant Hill villagers respected both holy and official holidays with punctiliousness. In 1842, the Sabbath fell on December 25, and the families observed the day with humility. The scribe wrote, "All in the Church (covenant-signed Shakers) partook of their breakfast on their knees." On Shaker holy days, after September of 1844, the villagers trekked to sacred Holy Sinai's Plain, a secluded place which they had set aside for special religious ceremonies.

Time moved on and events far removed from Pleasant Hill were to have a fundamental impact on the Society of Believers. On New Year's Day, 1861, no one at Pleasant Hill could have foreseen the disastrous events which would occur in the next two years. A visitor at that date may have seen the Shakers busily engaged in their traditional tasks. He would have heard the complaint that excess rain in June had injured the strawberry crop and that the traders were making their usual rounds selling Shaker products or attending Kentucky stock shows.

Little could the journalist have perceived that events of future months would lead to disruption of the traditional Shaker way of life at Pleasant Hill. The Civil War was the watershed in the village's history. Not only was the presence of the armies unsettling to morale and fortunes, the overall impact of the war and the ugly aftermath of radical Reconstruction were most devastating. Moreover, by the end of the war the village leadership had grown old and weary, and there were no young leaders coming on to take their place. The war destroyed the southern markets for Shaker products, and the rise of the new mechanical industrialization offered ruinous competition for Shaker craft skills.

By 1870, the Pleasant Hill journals reflected little more than the prosaic activities of a society which was rapidly losing its vitality. Gone from their pages was the vibrant spirit which had prevailed so strongly before the war. Bad management, unfortunate debts, and constantly dwindling membership clouded the dream of a way of life where human beings could live together in communal harmony. The last Shaker, Sister Mary Settles, died in 1923 and, like the faint ticking of a clock, the Society of Believers at Pleasant Hill wound down into oblivion as "Shakertown" assumed the characteristics of a typical Kentucky hamlet with gasoline stations and a general store. Shaker workshops became homes for local farmers and the voices raised in song at the Meeting House were from the congregation of the Shakertown Baptist Church.

However, there remains a spirit that hovers over Pleasant Hill and its landscape. No doubt the souls of early Shakers glory in the fact that the physical part of their dream is assured in perpetuity as a result of a private restoration effort begun in 1961 by the late Earl D. Wallace, Sr.

Today, purebred cattle still graze in the meadows, the plows still turn the soil, the cleaning chores are never-ending at the dwelling houses, and the cliff road still intimately links the village and the river. In a much more tangible fashion, rows of rock fences remain and many of the buildings, constructed with grace and integrity by Micajah Burnett and his laborers, are as useful today as when they were first built. Nearly 2700 acres of Shaker land have been preserved and thirty original buildings restored with meticulous care, down to faithfully duplicating the "original blue" paint trim. Today, Pleasant Hill is a National Historic Landmark and the largest of all restored Shaker villages.

As though the Shakers willed it, Pleasant Hill has been faithfully restored as a living monument to their quiet but ingenious society which sought to live its own particular way of life and is still a peaceful island in a sometimes turbulent world.

THOMAS D. CLARK

West Family Dwelling, 1821-1822.
Separate doorways for Shaker sisters and brethren were reminders of the vow of celibacy.

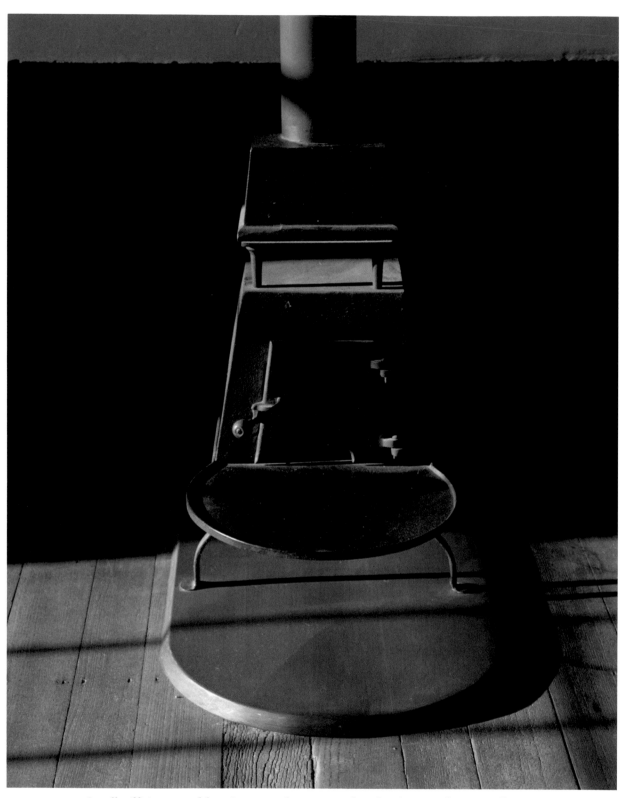

Small, efficient wood-burning stoves began to replace fireplaces at Pleasant Hill prior to 1820. The double chamber and tall stovepipe radiated additional heat. Reproductions, such as this, are fitted with gas burners to provide heat in Centre Family Dwelling.

The wooden hat form, with high crown and broad brim, defines a common style worn by Shaker brethren. Few of the fragile straw and felt hats have survived.

West bake kitchen, Centre Family Dwelling, 1824-1834.
The Shakers devised efficient ways to keep their dwellings and shops in perfect order,
such as the handsome built-in cupboards lining the bake room walls.

This view of Centre Family Dwelling, with the Meeting House beyond, accentuates the superbly-handled architectural mass of the dwelling.

Kentucky River palisades: "From its limestone shoulders the Shakers chiseled great blocks of stone and from its forested shores they harvested ever-increasing volumes of virgin timber with which to construct their buildings." Thomas D. Clark

The palisades of the Kentucky River provide a diverse environment for wild flora. Shaker Landing Road, descending 350 feet from the village to the river, is lined with abundant species of plant life. The waterfall is near the site of the Shakers' ferry and warehouses.

With perfection in architectural detail and proportion,
the appearance of the stone Centre Family Dwelling belies its enormous size.

East Family Dwelling, 1817,
was the first large residence built on the east-west village road.

Centre Family Dwelling.
Well-planned spaces and carefully-placed windows bring natural light into this
storage corner of the dwelling's kitchen.

Dining room, Centre Family Dwelling.
Backless benches at the tables were replaced by "boughten" chairs in the 1860s,
representing the encroachment of the world upon an aging population of Believers.

East Family Sisters' Shop, 1855. Kentucky Shakers were engaged
in a successful silk industry by the late 1830s. The second floor of the shop was used
for the labor-intensive care of silkworms during the feeding cycle each spring.

Farm Deacon's Shop, 1809.
The first permanent structure at Pleasant Hill, this stone dwelling replaced a
log residence of the Centre family.

West Lot Dwelling, 1826.
The West Lot family was a novitiate or gathering order, where individuals were
introduced to Shaker life. Intended as one step in a convert's spiritual "travel,"
in reality, the West Lot family became home to many who
could not make a commitment.

Border Leicester sheep, raised at Pleasant Hill today,
produce fine, long fleece. Washed wool is carded and spun in the East Family Sisters'
Shop, then warped on looms for weaving into shawls worn by village interpreters.

Cooper's Shop, 1847; East Family Wash House, circa 1825.
Cooper's ware appears among the earliest records of products made for sale.

Miles of fence—white picket, plank
and fieldstone—define the physical order of the Society's life at Pleasant Hill.

Ministry's dining room, Centre Family Dwelling.
A simply-laid table of utensils and plain ironstone. Said Mother Ann: "...Let your
table be clean enough to eat from without cloths."

Tall cupboards and chests and rows of pinrail are evidence of ordered living.

Founded. 1824.
Finished. 1825.

The forty-room Centre Family Dwelling
is the primary exhibition building in the restored village, where visitors are introduced
to the rich legacy of Pleasant Hill.

Retiring room, Centre Family Dwelling.
Believers were admonished to "retire to rest in the fear of God. . .and lie straight."

*Trustees' Office, 1839-1841. Built in the "outer court," the Trustees' Office was
the most worldly of Pleasant Hill structures. Here office deacons and trustees conducted
business with the "world's people," accommodated travelers and visiting Shakers.*

*Spiraling three floors, the twin staircases
of the Trustees' Office are supreme achievements of Pleasant Hill Shaker craftsmanship.*

Centre Family Dwelling.
The refined symmetry of Pleasant Hill architecture reflects Shaker daily life:
order, balance, utility and the equality, but separation, of the sexes.

*"On days when the Kentucky River thrusts up a gossamer of mist,
Pleasant Hill, with its collection of harmonious and simple buildings, assumes the
ethereal appearance of a floating island." Thomas D. Clark*

West Family shops.
Believers went to their tasks each day in well-lighted, well-ventilated workplaces
equipped with the most convenient and efficient tools.

East Family Dwelling stands near the intersection of the 1839
turnpike road and the Shakers' 1826 road to their landing on the Kentucky River.

Over 2700 acres of rolling bluegrass
countryside protect the restored village from modern development and enhance
the pastoral feeling of Pleasant Hill today.

North Lot Dwelling, circa 1816.
The frame dwelling is the sole survivor of the once-thriving novitiate family.

Centre Family Dwelling.
Neat, orderly and sparsely-furnished retiring rooms were for sleeping. The occupants of
this room spent the daylight hours at labor in shops, gardens, fields and kitchens.

Of the village buildings, the North Lot Dwelling remains on a public highway.

Along Shawnee Run Creek, the Society at Pleasant Hill
established an early industrial economy. Dams, sluices and springs created power
for a sawmill, gristmill, fulling mill and linseed oil mill.

Farm Deacon's Shop.

Tanyard Brick Shop, 1823.

West Family Sisters' Shop, 1844, and *West Family Dwelling, 1821-1822.*

Cooper's Shop and East Family Sisters' Shop.
Shaker workmen used different materials and forms in building their shops
and dwellings, but all bear the mark of simple elegance.

Meeting room, Centre Family Dwelling.
A perfection in light, sound and architecture, the room saw daily use. Singing meetings
and other family gatherings were part of the well-ordered Shaker day.

*Tanyard Brick Shop is the only structure that remains of the
Tanyard complex. Distanced from the center of village activity, Tanyard workers conducted
the smelly work of processing hides for use by cobblers, saddlers, and harness makers.*

Old Stone Shop, 1811,
was the first dwelling built for the West family. It was later used for medical offices.

Pleasant Hill Shakers cultivated herbs for their medicinal
properties and for dyes and seasonings. Far greater numbers and varieties of plants
were gathered in the fields, woods and along creek banks.

*"Today we began to haul stone to run a fence . . .
at the head of the big west pond; last spring their (sic) was 11 or 12 rods of fence
made to stop the earth from run(ning) in the pond, the sam(e) fence is now
to be continued on up to the pike." Pleasant Hill Journal, 1857.*

Pleasant Hill's Border Leicester flock.
Kentucky Shakers pioneered the development, in the West, of improved livestock.
Leicester or Bakewell sheep were imported from eastern New York soon after
their introduction to America in the 1820s.

*Dominating the village landscape, the Centre Family Dwelling is one of the
finest examples of Shaker construction, incorporating the best tradition of American
architecture with Shaker principles of honesty and excellence in workmanship.*

Water House, 1833, and Brethren's Bath House, 1860.
From the Tanyard spring, water was pumped underground by horsepower to a reservoir
within the Water House. This raised cypress tank fed water by gravity
flow to dwellings, barns, and wash houses.

Trustees' Office, Ministry's Workshop, and Meeting House
are seen from the Centre Family Dwelling roof. These structures were at the center
of temporal and spiritual village life.

The Meeting House was for Sunday worship in the
spacious first floor room. The Ministry had apartments above, their workshop nearby.

Arched windows and fanlight transoms are distinctive
Pleasant Hill features, reflecting their antecedents in worldly architectural traditions.

*A scarne holds spools of dyed yarn for ease in unwinding. The row of Shaker
spinning wheels recalls that the textile needs of the large community at Pleasant Hill
consumed thousands of yards of handspun thread.*

Centre Family Dwelling.

Ministry's Workshop, 1820.
Winter brought the Pleasant Hill Believers mainly to indoor pursuits that were
no less essential to community life.

High Bridge spans the gorge near Shaker Landing, 275 feet above the Kentucky River. During its construction in the 1870s, the engineering achievement was watched with interest by Pleasant Hill Shakers, who owned land on both sides of the river.

*Mist shrouds a twentieth-century barn
on the farmland surrounding the restored Shaker Village of Pleasant Hill.*

Tanyard Brick Shop.
The abundant water source in this valley attracted early settlement as a domestic site.

North Lot Dwelling, circa 1816.
Considered the "first outside family," the North Lot gathering order conducted their
affairs independently of the covenant-signed Shakers of Centre, East and West
families. "Out" or "outside" indicated their separation
both physically and spiritually.

*Ministry's dining room, Centre Family Dwelling. A small, frame addition
to the great stone dwelling served as a dining room for the ministry: two elders and two
eldresses, who were the appointed "leads" of the Pleasant Hill Society.*

*"For three-quarters of a century the saga of the Kentucky
River runs through Shaker journals in phrases of eloquent esteem."* Thomas D. Clark

*From 1816, when the Pleasant Hill Shakers
launched their first flatboat, until after the Civil War, the Kentucky River was the
Society's principal avenue of commerce.*

Early morning mist at High Bridge on the Kentucky River.

Brethren's Bath House.

The distinctive Shaker sisters' bonnets were made of palm leaf
or straw which was woven on a loom, then cut, shaped and sewn together.

"No other nineteenth-century Kentuckians were more
raptly attuned to the rhythms of the land and the seasonal changes. Their lives were
synchronized to the unfolding and dormancies of nature." Thomas D. Clark

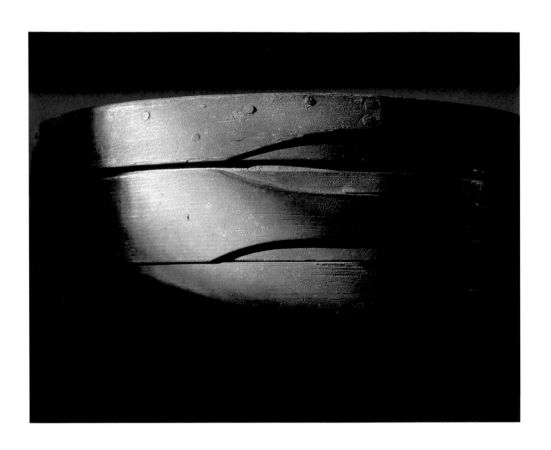

Family dwellings at Pleasant Hill had infirmaries,
or nurses' rooms, separated from the living areas of household occupants.

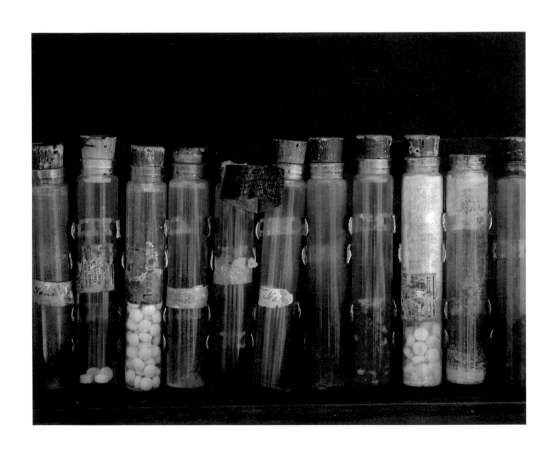

East Family Brethren's Shop, 1845; East Family Dwelling, 1817.
A gentle snowfall accentuates the stark geometry of Shaker architecture.

Light floods into interior storage areas of Centre Family Dwelling.
The Shakers' preoccupation with ventilation and light called for piercing the roof
line with dormers, admitting light into the dark attic spaces.

Boots and shoes were custom made for individual Believers.
Village account books record the number of pairs completed annually for each family
and the much smaller number produced for sale.

Meeting House, Ministry's Workshop, Trustees' Office.

In the Trustees' Office, business with "the world"
was conducted apart from the consecrated daily life of most Pleasant Hill Believers.

*A finely-made two-harness loom is representative of untold numbers
of looms used to produce all textiles for the community of nearly 500 Believers.*

A seemingly impenetrable barrier, the palisades were breached
as early as 1813 by Pleasant Hill Shakers. "Early this year . . . we made a waggon (sic)
road down the cliff on each side of the river. . . ." Pleasant Hill manuscript.

Modern-day cattle graze near the Tanyard Brick Shop.
Pleasant Hill was one Shaker community where farming remained the mainstay of
village economy. Today, agriculture plays a role in supporting the preservation
effort of the nonprofit corporation.

Centre Family Dwelling.
The year-around serenity of Pleasant Hill takes on a special quality in winter.

Pure white, even to trim and shutter, the Meeting House was at the heart of Shaker life.

Identical limestone markers at each Shaker grave site
bear only initials. A few late stones differ from earlier ideas of anonymity and simplicity.

East Family Sisters' Shop.
At early morning light, sisters were already diligently working on assigned tasks:
sewing, spinning, weaving fine baskets or tending silkworms.

Restrained in design, precise in details,
chairs echo the harmony of architecture and furnishings at Pleasant Hill.

The number of surviving spit boxes is evidence that Believers
persisted in the use of tobacco, despite a prohibition issued in the 1840s.

The West Family corn crib, 1854,
represents the dozens of functional buildings essential to an agrarian community.

Fence pickets were created in shops where Shaker-designed
machines and devices made repetitive work more efficient. A Believer's time and
talent were God-given resources worthy of conservation.

INDEX

THE GIFT OF PLEASANT HILL

Designed by Susan Jackson Keig
Composed by DigiType, Inc. in Garamond
with display lines in Modern 216 by Ull-tra Typographers, Inc.
Printed by Jones Printing Company, Inc.
on Potlatch Northwest Quintessence 100lb. dull enamel text
with endsheets of Simpson Sundance 80lb. text
Bound by Nicholstone Company, Inc.
in International Coatings Group, Inc. Arrestox B
and stamped in silver foil